# Contents

# Franklin D. Roosevelt

Sandra Woodcock

Published in association with The Basic Skills Agency

## Hodder & Stoughton

A MEMBER OF THE HODDER HEADLINE GROUP

**Acknowledgements**

Photos: pp. 3, 7, 10, 13, 25 © Corbis-Bettmann,
        p. 20 © Hulton Deutsch Collection,
        p. 23 © Hulton Getty Collection.
Cover photo: © Hulton Getty Collection.

Orders: please contact Bookpoint Ltd, 39 Milton Park, Abingdon, Oxon OX14 4TD. Telephone: (44) 01235 400414, Fax: (44) 01235 400454. Lines are open from 9.00–6.00, Monday to Saturday, with a 24 hour message answering service. Email address: orders@bookpoint.co.uk

British Library Cataloguing in Publication Data
A catalogue record for this title is available from The British Library

ISBN 0 340 71162 0

First published 1998
Impression number 10 9 8 7 6 5 4 3 2 1
Year 2003 2002 2001 2000 1999 1998

Copyright © 1998 Sandra Woodcock

Typeset by Fakenham Photosetting Ltd, Fakenham, Norfolk.
Printed in Great Britain for Hodder & Stoughton Educational, a division of Hodder Headline Plc, 338 Euston Road, London NW1 3BH by Page Bros Ltd, Norwich.

# 1 Early Life

Franklin Roosevelt was born in 1882.
He was an only child.
His parents were well off.
They lived in New York in a pleasant house.

Life was happy for the young boy.
He spent a lot of time outdoors.
He loved nature and outdoor sports.
He liked swimming and sailing best.
He also liked reading and stamp collecting.

In the summer holidays,
the family often went to Europe.
Young Franklin could speak
both French and German.

At school and at college he was a good student.

When he was 23,
he married a girl called Eleanor.
She was a distant cousin.

His mother did not want him to marry.
She did not want to lose her son.
She was difficult for many years.
But Eleanor learned to put up with
her mother-in-law.

Roosevelt trained to be a lawyer.
But he soon lost interest in this.

He went into politics,
and helped to run the US navy.

He was good at his job
and people soon got to know him.
He was tall, good looking
and made friends easily.

In 1921 he became very ill.
Doctors said he had polio.
He was in great pain and could not walk.
Polio left him crippled.

He saw many doctors.
He tried exercises,
and did lots of swimming.
But it was no good.
For the rest of his life,
he could not walk without help.

His mother wanted him to give up work
and live a quiet life at home.
But Roosevelt would not give up.

His wife stood by him
and helped him as much as she could.

Roosevelt never regained
the use of his legs.
He set up a charity to help
other polio victims.

He was also the head of
the 'March of Dimes' program.
This program was set up to
find a cure for polio.
In time, it found a vaccine
for the disease, wiping out polio for ever.

With help from his wife,
Roosevelt went on with
his career in politics.
He became one of the best loved
leaders of America.

# 2 'Boom and Bust'

In the 1920s, America was 'booming'.
These years are sometimes called
the 'Roaring Twenties'.
American industry was doing well.

Many people had lots of money to spend.
Some people became very rich.
But all this came to an end in 1929.

There was a crash on the stock market.
Many people, who had bought shares,
lost everything.

People lost confidence
and would not put their money into business.
Factories closed down,
and people lost their jobs.
Many firms went bankrupt.

A man begging for food in America in the 1930s.

The banks stopped lending money,
so business could not recover.
More people lost their jobs.

Many people were now too poor
to pay their rent, or even buy food.

At that time,
the government did not pay benefits
to people out of work.

Many people had to live on the streets
and beg for food.
America seemed to hit rock bottom.
The leaders had no way out.
They had no answers.

Roosevelt was different.
He did have ideas to
get America out of the mess.

In 1932, Roosevelt asked the people
of America to vote for him as President.
He said the people must get over their fear
and have confidence again.

He promised a 'New Deal' for the people.

Roosevelt went to
as many States as he could.
He made speeches every night.
He was popular everywhere he went.
The people liked him and trusted him.
He smiled, he was confident,
and he gave them hope.

Roosevelt won a great victory.
He won by seven million votes.
In 1933, he became President of America.
He told the people:
'The only thing we have to fear,
is fear itself'.

Roosevelt campaigning in 1932.

# 3 President

Now that he was President,
Roosevelt began to deal with
America's problems.
He had new ideas,
new ways of doing things.

He said that the government must spend money
to help the country recover.
In the next five years,
many new laws came in.

Roosevelt said the first step was to
help the unemployed and their families.
He gave money to the States to do this.

The government set up new projects
to build power stations,
schools and other public buildings.

Some unemployed men went to live and work
in special outdoor camps.
They were given food and shelter.
They were able to send most of their
pay home to their families.

Roosevelt took action to
help farmers and business men.
He wanted the poor to have
help from the government.

He started old age pensions
and unemployment pay.
There were laws to make wages fair.
Roosevelt's plans for all these things
were called 'The New Deal'.

Franklin Roosevelt with his wife, Eleanor.

Some people did not like the New Deal.
They did not like the government
spending money in these ways.

Some said Roosevelt was a traitor
to his own social class,
because he helped the poor.

It was his own energy and will power
that pushed the New Deal.
Without the New Deal,
many Americans would have starved.
They could not afford to eat.

But slowly in the 1930s,
America began to recover.
The people voted for Roosevelt to be
the President three more times.
He won again in 1936, 1940 and 1944.

# 4 World War Two

In the 1930s,
there were many dangers to world peace.
In Europe, Hitler was a danger to peace.
Many people in America said
this was not their business.
They said that America should
stay out of it.

Roosevelt did not think like this.
He was worried about war.
He said that America should use its power
to stop war happening.

He used government money
to build up the navy.
When war began in Europe in 1939,
Roosevelt did all he could
to help Britain and France.
He sold weapons to them, he lent them money.

By 1941, America was not at war
with Germany.
But America was doing everything possible
to help Britain.

Roosevelt met the British leader,
Winston Churchill,
on a ship in the Atlantic ocean.
They signed the 'Atlantic Charter'.
It said the people of the world
must be set free from fear.

But still, America was not at war.

In the East, Japan was trying to
build up its power.
America's navy could stop them.
The leaders of Japan did not want this.

The bombing of Pearl Harbor, in December 1941.

Japan was not at war with America.
But in December 1941,
they bombed the American navy,
at the naval base in Pearl Harbor.

Now Roosevelt took America to war.
Germany was allied to Japan,
so now America was at war
with Germany as well.

It was a World War.

# 5 World Leader

Roosevelt was now a world leader
in the fight against Hitler.

There were three main leaders
in the war against Hitler.
They were known as the 'Big Three'.

They were:
Churchill in Britain,
Stalin in Russia and Roosevelt in America.

These 'Big Three' had meetings in Europe
to plan how they would deal with the war.
Roosevelt needed all his energy.

The 'Big Three': Stalin, Roosevelt and Churchill.

As a war leader,
he had to win the American people to his side.
He had to show them
that they could not keep out of this war.

In 1945 it was clear that
Germany would be beaten.
The Big Three began to think
about what would happen after the war.

What would happen to Germany?
What would happen to Europe?
How much power would Russia have?
How much power would Britain have,
when the war ended?

Roosevelt put a lot into these talks.

At one meeting, they agreed to set up
the United Nations when the war was over.

The 'Declaration of the United Nations'
was signed on 1 January 1942.

In this declaration,
all the countries fighting against Hitler
agreed to keep the peace after the war.

No-one wanted to have another war
like World War Two.

Roosevelt was worried
about the power the British would have
once the war was over.
Others were worried about the
Russian leader, Joseph Stalin.

Churchill said that Stalin would try
to take Communism into Europe
when Germany was beaten.

Roosevelt got on well with Stalin
when he met him.
He thought Stalin could be trusted.

Roosevelt did not live to see
the end of World War Two.
The war had put a great strain on him.

The war in Europe ended on 8 May 1945.
The World finally saw full peace when
Japan surrendered on 2 September 1945.

But Roosevelt did not live to see
either of these great days.
He died in April 1945,
from a massive stroke.

But his work lives on.
Even in the 1990s,
the United Nations tries to make peace
between countries which are at war.

Roosevelt was the only man to be elected
as President of America four times.
America has had many great Presidents.
But Roosevelt was one of the most popular.